Introduction To Peking Opera

Jing

By Zhou Chuanjia

Illustrated by Pangbudun'er

RC

Books Beyond Boundaries

ROYAL COLLINS

Jing characters are what we usually call the "big painted faces." Their name is *Jing*, which means "clean," but their faces are not clean at all. How many different face-makeup combinations do they have? Let's check it out!

Li Kui

Green-Face Tiger

Hei Fengli

Ma Wu

Lu Zhishen

Yuchi Gong

Xu Yanzhao

Lord Bao

The Gigantic River God

Yu Hong

Zhang Fei

Wen Zhong

Shan Xiongxin

Li Qi

Yao Qi

Cao Cao

5

Purple Big Dragon Robe

Dragon robe is a type of official uniform for people of high status like emperors, kings, generals, and prime ministers. There are different colors too, such as red, yellow, green, white, black, and purple. *Jing* characters usually wear big dragon robes.

Jade Belt

The jade belt goes with the dragon robe and other official uniforms. It shows that people wearing it are important.

Prime Minister's Gauze Cap

This is for the prime minister in a play only.

Fenyang **Helmet**

Also called the *wenyang* helmet. This is for prime ministers as well.

Thick Boots

Bound Headdress

This is usually worn by warriors.

Black *Kao* Armor

Kao armor is what generals wear in wars.
Different characters will wear different colors
(e.g., red, yellow, green, white, and black).
The color of one's armor also indicates a
character's personality.

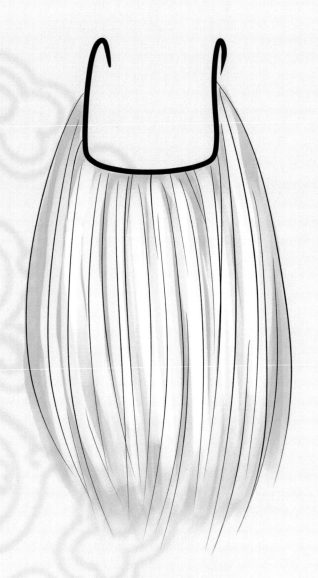

White Beard (full beard)

Red Beard (side beard)

The false beard in Peking Opera is called *rankou*. The full beard, or "full," covers the actor's mouth completely. The actors will choose to wear a full beard that comes in the color black, white, and grey according to the age of the character they are playing; for example, the beard for Lord Bao is black. The side beard, or "side," is also like a full beard except it doesn't cover the actor's mouth. The *Jing* characters with side beards are brave and hot-tempered fighters, like Ma Wu and Shan Xiongxin. Both of them wear a red "side".

9

Main *Jing*

These *Jing* characters have a lot of singing performances. They are also called "painted face with a brass hammer" or "black faces."

Facial Makeup

Xu Yanzhao's makeup is mainly purple. This color represents integrity and composure. You can see the makeup exaggerates the shape of the actor's eyebrows, with the purple part taking up sixty percent of the facial area and the white part taking up forty percent. Makeup with this kind of color divide is also called "old face" – meaning it is suitable for old characters.

Xu Yanzhao in *Saving the Throne*

In *Saving the Throne*, Lord Protector Xu Yanzhao takes a small brass hammer with him on stage. Before the old emperor died, he bestowed Xu this brass hammer so that he could "hit" (metaphorically of course) unqualified young emperors as well as evil ministers. Because Xu is a famous *Jing* character who mainly sings, people remember him and his brass hammer well and began to call all singing *Jing* characters by the name "painted face with a brass hammer."

Facial Makeup

This is Lord Bao's makeup. Black represents loyalty, selflessness, and uprightness. For this type of makeup, actors will first paint their whole face in one color (black for Lord Bao), and then they will use another color to emphasize their eyebrows, eyes, mouth, and nose. For Lord Bao, actors will also paint a crescent on their forehead, either facing left or right. According to the legend, Lord Bao was such a just and honest judge that he could "put any human to trial during the day and put any ghost to trial during the night."

Lord Bao in *Beheading Chen Shimei*

There are a lot of plays with Lord Bao in them, such as *Beheading Chen Shimei*, *Chisang Town*, and *The Ghost's Testimoney*. Like Xu Yanzhao, Lord Bao is also a well-known *Jing* singer, so people begin to refer to other singing *Jing* characters as "black faces" because of Lord Bao's signature black face-makeup.

Yao Qi and Wen Zhong are also important Main *Jing* characters.

Facial Makeup

Yao Qi has a white face with a black cross. The actors will paint a black line that goes from the tip of the nose to the forehead. Because the actors' eye sockets, temples, and chins are also painted black, it looks like they have a black cross in the middle of their face.

Yao Qi in *Hitting the Golden Brick*

Facial Makeup

Do you see any similarity between Wen Zhong's makeup and that of Xu Yanzhao which we saw earlier? They have the same color division with the upper part taking up forty percent and the lower part taking up sixty percent. Wen Zhong's makeup is red, with a "spiritual third eye" on his forehead. This means he can distinguish good from evil.

Wen Zhong in *Grand Triumphant Return*

13

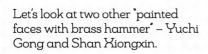

Let's look at two other "painted faces with brass hammer" – Yuchi Gong and Shan Xiongxin.

Face Makeup

Yuchi Gong's makeup is in black and white, and the black takes up sixty percent of the face. This color not only shows that Yuchi Gong has very dark skin but also shows he is an honest and brave person.

Yuchi Gong in *Reunion of Father and Son*

14

Facial Makeup

Shan Xiongxin has a blue face with small colorful decorations. Blue represents bravery and a clever, scheming character. The blue color takes up most of the makeup, but there are lines and stripes painted in multiple colors around the facial features. That's why this kind of makeup is also called "sprinkled face paint."

Shan Xiongxin in *Defeating the Five Kings*

Beheading Chen Shimei

During the Song Dynasty (10th–13th century), a scholar called Chen Shimei ranked first in the national imperial exam one year, so the emperor married his daughter to him. But Chen didn't tell anyone that he was already married and had two children. When his wife Qin Xianglian and their children came to the capital to look for him, Chen not only refused to meet with them, but he also sent an assassin to murder them. Qin Xianglian reported her husband to Lord Bao, the most virtuous judge. Although the princess and the empress – Chen's new wife and mother-in-law – threatened Lord Bao with his career and his life, Lord Bao didn't fear their authority; he eventually beheaded the cruel and ungrateful Chen Shimei.

Acting *Jing*

Different from singing *Jing*, these characters focus mainly on movement, dialogue, and acting performances. They are brave, reckless, simple, and humorous. Some examples are Ma Wu in *Hitting the Golden Brick*, Jiang Wei in *Mount Tielong*, the "Green-Face Tiger" in *White Water Beach*. When they feel happy, excited, angry, or confident, they will express their emotions by shouting "Wa Yaa Yaaa—" Have you ever heard it?

Facial Makeup

Ma Wu's makeup is also a blue "sprinkled face paint." But the patterns are different from Shan Xiongxin's makeup.

Ma Wu in *Hitting the Golden Brick*

Facial Makeup

Cao Cao's makeup is white. We call it "watery-white face." Characters with a watery-white face are usually evil and suspicious, like Cao Cao. Another type of white face-makeup is "oily white face." These characters are usually arrogant, like Ma Su.

Cao Cao in *Battle of Wancheng*

Facial Makeup

Lu Zhishen is a Buddhist monk so his makeup is called the "monk's makeup." The actors playing Lu Zhishen will paint their eye sockets in the shape of distorted ellipses, and they will paint small patterns around their noses and mouths. On their foreheads, they will also paint a Buddhist relic bead or nine dots to show this character is a Buddhist disciple.

Lu Zhishen *in Yezhu Forest*

Facial Makeup

Li Qi's makeup is called "distorted makeup." It emphasizes awkwardness and ugliness of the character by purposefully making the facial features asymmetrical. Li Qi is a criminal, so he wears the criminal's costume and shackles on his hands and feet.

Li Qi in *The Bandit's Regret*

21

Facial Makeup

Li Kui also has "cross" makeup. The black paint goes straight from the top of the forehead to the bottom of the chin.

Li Kui in *Li Kui Visits his Mother*

Facial Makeup

Zhang Fei's "cross" makeup is called "butterfly face." It makes him appear cheerful and smiley, but at the same time it also gives him a fierce and gallant look like a cheetah.

Zhang Fei in *Reunion at Gucheng*

Cao Cao's Insult Turned Against Him

In the Three Kingdoms Period (3rd century), a reputed scholar, Mi Heng, was introduced to the King of Wei, Cao Cao. Cao didn't take Mi seriously and insulted him by letting him take care of the drum in court. Mi Heng was very angry, and he hit the drum loudly and reproached Cao in front of everyone. Cao was so infuriated that he wanted to kill him; many people pleaded on Mi's behalf, so Cao gave Mi another task and sent him away.

Martial *Jing*

Also called "secondary martial arts face paint" or "fighting face paint." These characters only perform fighting movements without any singing or dialogue.

The "Green-Face Tiger" in *White Water Beach*

The Gigantic River God in *Havoc in Heaven*

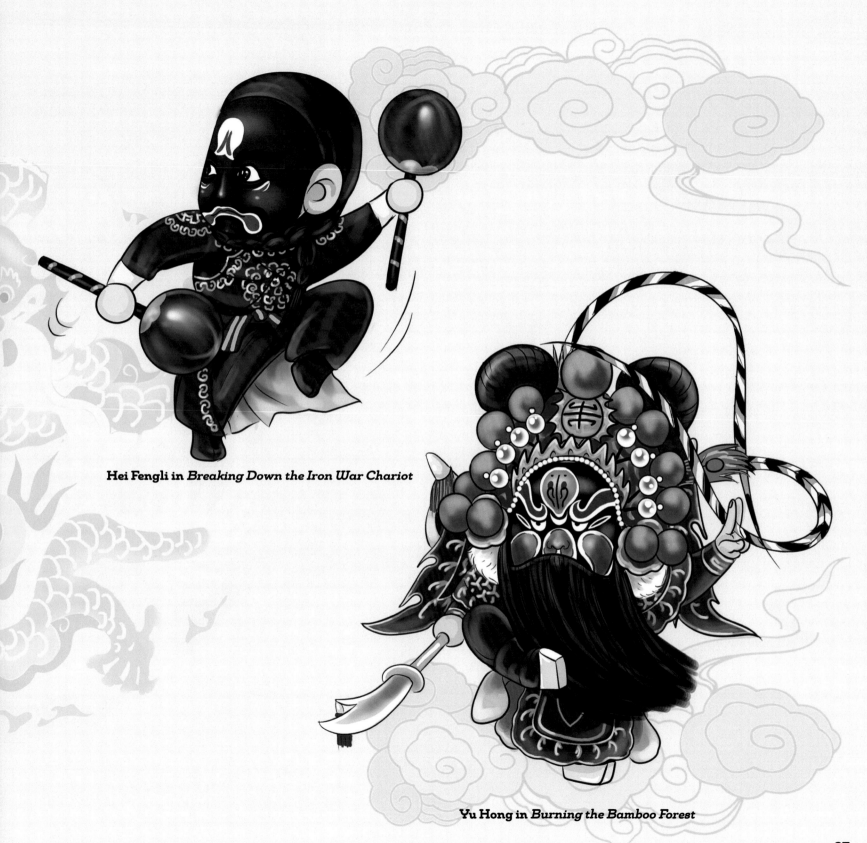

Hei Fengli in *Breaking Down the Iron War Chariot*

Yu Hong in *Burning the Bamboo Forest*

27

White Water Beach

The "Green-Face Tiger" Xu Qiying – a heroic outlaw and leader of the stockaded village on Leopard Mountain – was arrested by government soldiers. He was being escorted to the capital by Liu Renjie, the army commander's son, when his sister, Xu Peizhu, led their village troops to attack the government army. A servant of the Cheng family called Shiyi saw the fight and thought a group of bandits were robbing the soldiers. So, he helped Liu and his men drive the "Green-Face Tiger" and his sister away.

However, the ungrateful Liu didn't thank Shiyi for saving his life. Instead, he was afraid that the government would blame him for letting the "Green-Face Tiger" get away, so he blamed Shiyi and put him in jail. The Cheng family that Shiyi served in was also accused of helping the bandits, and they were banished from the country. On their way, the family met the "Green-Face Tiger" and his sister, and they told this sad story. When the Xu brother and sister heard how the innocent Cheng family and Shiyi suffered because of them, they put on a disguise and rescued Shiyi from the execution ground.

Jiang Wei from *Mount Tielong*. Red represents loyalty and bravery.

Yuwen Chengdu in *Nanyang Pass*. Yellow represents ferocity and aggressiveness.

Cheng Yaojin in *Jia's Wine House*. Green represents toughness and recklessness.

Dou Erdun in *Stealing the Royal Horse*. Blue represents strength and bravery.

Lu Zhishen

Let's learn more about Peking Opera (3)

Zhou Chuanjia – professor at Beijing Union University and researcher at the Central Research Institute of Culture and History.

The *Jing* category

Jing is also referred to as "face paint" because the actors wear bright colorful makeup on their faces. Their performance is theatrical and their singing style is sonorous. The characters they play are usually brave, reckless, and sometimes violent. There are three main sub-categories in this role: the Brass-Hammer *Jing*, Acting *Jing*, and Martial *Jing*.

Brass-Hammer *Jing* emphasizes singing in its performance and usually interprets righteous high ministers and military officers. A typical character in this role is Xu Yanzhao in *Saving the Throne, Entreating Ancestor's Blessing, Requesting a Second Audience*. The brass hammer he carries on stage later becomes an identifier for other *Jing* characters, including: Ji Liao in *Assassinating the Prince*, Shan Xiongxin in *Defeating the Five Kings*, Yang Yansi in *Martyr Brothers*, Gao Wang in *Battle at Muhu Pass*.

Also, because there are several characters with signature black makeup, we also refer to them as "Black-Face *Jing*." Some famous "Black Faces" are: Lord Bao in *Chisang Village, Beheading Chen Shimei*, and *The Ghost's Testimony*, Yuchi Gong in *Reunion of Father and Son, Foul Play*, and *The Mad General*, Yao Qi in *Defying the Death Penalty*.

Acting *Jing* emphasizes acting and dialogue in its performance. The characters interpreted are various, including civil ministers, military generals, heroes, and bullies – both old and young. Examples are: Dou Erdun in *Stealing the Royal Horse*, Ma Su in *Battle of Jieting*, Yao Gang in *Killing the Bully*, Li Qi in *The Bandit's Regret*, Lu Zhishen in *Yezhu Forest*, Zhang Dingbian in *Loyal General Officer*, Bao Zian in *Enemy Becomes Family*, Zheng Ziming in *Executing the Yellow Robe*.

In addition, there is also Zhang Fei, Li Kui, Jiao Zan, Ma Wu, Niu Gao, who appear in these plays too. Other characters wearing white makeup such as Cao Cao, Yan Song, Pan Hong, Zhao Gao, Gu Du, Yi Li, Liu Jin, Wang Zhen, and Zhou Jianjun are also included.

Martial *Jing* characters are normally vulgar and adept fighters. Some plays were originally tailored for Martial *Jing* actors, but gradually Martial *Sheng* actors began to star in them as well. The characters in these plays that can be considered both Martial *Jing* and Martial *Sheng* include: Gao Deng in *Damsel in Distress*, Jiang Wei in *Mount Tielong*, Chang Yuchun in *The Champion*, the Leopard demon in *Leopard*, Li Yuanba in *Like Knows Like and Rescuing the Emperor*, Yang Yansi in *Battle of Jinshatan*, Bao Zian in *Chaos at the Jiaxing Court*, Fei Degong in *Temple Gathering*, Dian Wei in *Battle of Wancheng*.

If the martial arts character is the play lead, then it will be played by Martial *Jing* actors. For example, Jin Wushu in *Breaking Down the Iron War Chariot* and *Battle of Jinshan*, Yang Jian in *Feast of Imperial Peach* and *Havoc in Heaven*, Guan Sheng in *Defeating General Guan* and *Conquering the Liangshan Marsh*, Chi Fushou in *Defeat at Jinling*, Yu Hong in *The Martial Wife Fights Her Husband's War*, An Dianbao in *The Battle at Dumu Pass*. They wear long armor and archery cloaks. Another type of Martial *Jing* character is called "Fighting Face Paint." They wear short tight outfits. Examples are: the "Green-Face Tiger" in *White Water Beach*, Yu Hong in *Burning the Bamboo Forest*, Hei Fengli in *Breaking Down the Iron War Chariot*, Wu Wenhua in *Wujia Hills*, Liao Yin in *Ghost Lover*. Actors playing these roles perform a lot of martial arts and the fighting acts can be very intense.

Finally, there is a special sub-category called *Mao Jing*, or the "Oily Painted-Face." For example, Zhong Kui, Zhou Cang, the Great Demon God, the God of Justice, and the Gigantic River God. Usually, these characters are played by Acting *Jing* or Martial *Jing*.

About the Author:

Zhou Chuanjia was born in 1944. He studied at Peking University and Chinese National Academy of Arts, where he received his doctorate in literature. Zhou is a professor at Beijing Union University, a researcher at the Central Research Institute of Culture and History, and an expert who enjoys the special allowance of the State Council. Zhou has been teaching and researching Chinese literature, opera history, and opera critique for a long time. His major publications include *Introduction to Opera Script Writing, Performance of Famous Dan Actors*, and *Opera: Chinese Cultural Elements*.

About the Illustrator:

Pangbudun'er is an independent writer and painter of the post-80s generation. His work is engaging with its own unique style. He painted illustrations for *Fun Talks on the Three Kingdoms* by Cai Kangyong and Hou Wenyong; his other publications include *Raising the Curtains: Will you Hear Some Peking Opera?* and several Peking Opera picture books such as *Protecting the Protected* and *Empty Fort Strategy*.

Introduction To Peking Opera:
Jing

By Zhou Chuanjia
Illustrated by Pangbudun'er

First published in 2022 by Royal Collins Publishing Group Inc.
Groupe Publication Royal Collins Inc.
BKM Royalcollins Publishers Private Limited

Headquarters: 550-555 boul. René-Lévesque O Montréal (Québec) H2Z1B1 Canada
India office: 805 Hemkunt House, 8th Floor, Rajendra Place, New Delhi 110 008

Original Edition © Changchun Publishing House Co., Ltd.

ISBN: 978-1-4878-0913-3

To find out more about our publications, please visit www.royalcollins.com.